T0129875

Litany
of
Hope

Nkatha Kabira

authorHOUSE®

AuthorHouse™
1663 Liberty Drive
Bloomington, IN 47403
www.authorhouse.com
Phone: 1 (800) 839-8640

Published by AuthorHouse 10/20/2018

ISBN: 978-1-5462-6488-0 (sc)
ISBN: 978-1-5462-6487-3 (e)

Library of Congress Control Number: 2018912444

Print information available on the last page.

New International Version (NIV)
Copyright © 1973, 1978, 1984, 2011 by Biblica

ACKNOWLEDGMENTS

Deepest thanks to my family for always believing in me.

Thanks to my mother, Prof. Wanjiku M. Kabira - my teacher, my mentor, my inspiration, my role model and my biggest fan.

Thanks to my father, Dr. Jackson Kabira, for inspiring us to pursue what we love wholeheartedly.

Thanks to my sisters:

Wairimu, thank you for being our beacon of hope. Wambui, for your courageous spirit, Karambu, for your loving and devoted spirit.

And to my brother, Muturia, for your willpower and courage.

Thanks to all the places and communities that continue to fill me with hope – St. John Bosco Choir, Vincentian Ministries, Pentecostal Tabernacle, Cleveland Ministries, Hope Hub and STIAS.

Thanks also to Anna Su, Namita Wahi, Beatrice Ouma, Phylis Temea and Flora Ntuli for walking this journey of hope with me.

Thank you all.

Thank you, Lord.

To anyone and everyone who has ever had to wait.

And

To My Sun.

This **hope** does not disappoint us.

For God has poured out his love into our hearts through the Holy Spirit, who is God's gift to us.

Romans 5:5

The Bible, New International Version

CONTENTS

For I know the plans I have for you, declares the Lord, plans to prosper you and not to harm you, plans to give you **hope** and a future.

Jeremiah 29:11

The Bible, New International Version

The Long Journey Home

Our Father in heaven,
You who commanded light to shine
And it shone,
You who separated light from darkness
And called them day and night,
You who separated life below and above the water
And called them the skies and the seas,
You who commanded the earth to produce
And the earth produced all kinds of vegetation,
You who separated seasons
And commanded them to shine on earth,
You who commanded the oceans to be full of creatures
And commanded birds to fly,
You who commanded the earth to be full of animals,
You who filled the earth with men and women who
would rule over all of creation,
You who created the heavens and the earth,
You who feeds the birds in the air,
You who makes the stars light up in the skies,
You who promised me my Sun.

Generation after generation,
Season after season.

Beckoned,
Prayed,
Fasted,
Hoped,
Waited,

For I knew that you are a faithful God,
For I knew that you are not a man who would lie,
For I knew that your plans for me were good,
For I knew that your plans for me were to prosper me.

Our Father in heaven,
You put these desires into my heart.
You created this longing in my soul.
You composed this song that must be sung.
You are the poet who penned this poem.
You wrote those words that must be fulfilled.

Your kingdom arise,
Not my will but yours.
You willed it, Lord.
You decreed it, Lord,
And it shall surely come to pass
No matter how long it takes,
The long journey home.

27.6.2014

GOD'S WAYS

Faith or fear?

I can't tell.

I'm afraid
I can't understand your ways.
I'm afraid
I can't comprehend.
I'm afraid
I can't control.
I'm afraid.
But why, Lord?
I'm afraid
It looks like a mess, Lord.
I'm afraid.
Your methods, Lord, your methods.
I want to have faith, Lord.

Faith or fear?

Every day is a challenge

Lord, I surrender to you.

I want to trust your ways.
I want to trust your timings.
I want to believe your Word.
I want to hold onto your promises.

Faith or fear?

Lord, I choose faith.
A spirit of faith quenches fear.
A spirit of trust quenches fear.
A spirit of faith quenches it.

Lord, I trust you.

2.7.2015

God's Heart

I know His heart,
And He knows mine.
Through the eyes, I see
I am all I am.
Through the eyes, he sees
He is all that he is.
Through the eyes, she sees
He is all that he is.
Through the eyes, she sees
She is all that she is.
Consubstantial with the Father,
We are one,
God's heart.

2.7.2014

YOUR HEART

I hear it.

      I feel it.

          I see it.

              I know it.

                  I remember it.

                  I hear it beating.

                  I feel it feeling.

                  I see it moving.

                            I know it.

                            I know it.

                            I know it.

I remember it well.

          Your heart.

                        14.7.2014

HIS HE[ART]

Her art,   His art,
    Her heart.   His heart.
        His   Her
           Art,   Art,
             His   Her
               Heart.   Heart.

His art, his heart.   His art, his heart.
Her art, her heart.   Her art, her heart.

Her heart's art.   His heart's art.
     His heart,   Her heart,
His art's heart.   Her art's heart.
     His art,   His art,
Her art's heart.   His art's heart.
     His art's heart,   Her art's heart,
His heart's art.   Her heart's art.
     Her art.   His art.

His heart's art, her heart.
Her art's heart, his art.
His art's heart, her art's heart.
Her heart's art, his art.

God's heart.

9.7.2014

HE LOVES US

He

       loves

her

       He

loves

       him.

He

her.

loves

He loves her.

He loves her.

He loves her.

He loves her.   He loves him.

He loves her.   He loves him.

He loves her.   He loves him.

He loves us.

He loves us.

He loves us.

Oh, love.

11:11

He visited
One cold, wintry night.

He visited.
11:11.

I recognized.

He spoke
In a soft, whispery voice.

I noticed.

He answered
That cold, wintry night.

I knew.

He visited.
He answered.
He spoke.

I heard him.

12.6.2014

Promise Keeper

Our Father in heaven,
You who nourishes the birds in the sky,
You who created the heavens and the earth,
You who knew us before the foundations of the world,
You who keeps your promises,
You who promised Abraham he
would be the father of nations,
You who promised Moses he would
deliver the Israelites,
You who promised Joseph he would be king,
You who promised Jacob he would
take Rachel as his wife,
You who promised Mary she would
bring forth the King,
You who parted the Red Sea,
You who saved Daniel from the den of lions,
How much more will you give to us?
Our father in paradise,
We know where we belong.
You willed it, and it will be so.
We are on our way home.

12.6.2014

God's Love

He loves you
Not because of your philosophical self.
He loves you
Not because of your metaphysical self.
He loves you
Not because of your make-believe self.
He loves you
Not because of your theoretical self.
He loves you
Not because of your practical self.
He loves you.
He just loves you.
He adores you.
He cherishes you.
He just loves you
Just the way you are.

7.28.2014

FOR ALWAYS

I know you.
I remember you.
Nothing changed anything.
Everything changed nothing.
Nothing changed everything.
I know you.
I remember you
Always.

6.16.2015

ABBA FATHER

Lord God,

Creator
Of
The heavens,

I

Your

Humble

Servant

Surrender

Myself

To

You,

Mind,
Heart,
Body,
Soul.

I

Your

Faithful

Servant

Surrender

Myself

To

Your

Will

Through

Christ,

Amen.

9.1.2014

THE LORD SPOKE TO ME

My Lord,
I hear you.

> Fear not. I will help you.
> I will give you treasures out of the darkness.
> I will give you the crown of life.
> Fear not. I am with you.

My Lord,
I hear you.

> Fear not. I will help you.
> I will give you beauty out of the ashes.
> I will give you the crown of life.
> Fear not. I am with you.

My Lord,
I hear you.

> Fear not. I will help you.
> I will give you hope out of the pain.
> I will give you the crown of life.
> Fear not. I am with you.

My Lord,
I trust you.

19.8.2018

Canticle of Praise

For this wonderful day,
Lord, I thank you.
For your goodness,
Lord, I thank you.
For your faithfulness,
Lord, I thank you.
For your love,
Lord, I thank you.

Alpha and Omega,
Beginning and the end,
King of kings,
Queen of queens,
Lord of lords,
Prince of peace,
Creator Goddess,

For this wonderful day,
Lord, I thank you.
For your goodness,
Lord, I thank you.
For your faithfulness,
Lord, I thank you.
For your love,
Lord, I thank you.

For your mercy,
Lord, I thank you.

4.27.2015

LITANY OF THANKSGIVING

Lord,
You are good,
Divine,
Merciful.
Lord,
You are worthy of all praises.
Glory,
Praise,
Thanksgiving
Unto You.
Who is able?
Supremely,
Abundantly,
More than we ask for
Or
Imagine.
Thank
You,
Lord.

19.1.2015

ARISE

The Lord remembers
His promise forever.
The Lord's Word
Stands as solid as rock.

Arise,

Past,
Present,
Future

Generations,

Arise.

Fear not.
The Lord remembers
His promises forever.

May the sun set
On all that is not in accordance
With his holy will and purpose.

May the sun rise—*arise*.
In the north,
Truth north,
Generations await.

Arise.

28.12.2014

LITANY OF HOPES AND DREAMS

On this the first day
Of
The
Year
Of
Hopes and dreams

May I have the courage
To be the person
You have called me
To be.

May I be called

Woman of hope,
Woman of faith,
Woman of courage,
Woman of purpose.

Arise,

Daughter of God.

Awaken.

Your destiny awaits.

1.1.2015

LOVE

To love
Or not
To love?

The search,
The wondering,
The pain,
The wilderness,
The struggle.

From the beginning of time
His will was
For us to love.

I found him whom my soul loved
That I may love him.
I may cooperate with God's will.

His holy will
Was and is
To love.

29.11.2014

I Hate You with Love

My Sun,

Hating you is painful.

My Sun,

Hating you is unbearable.

My Sun,

I love hating you.

My Sun,

I hate loving you.

My Sun,

This hate I feel for you is love.

My Sun,

I hate you with love

Always.

30.7.2018

Her Heart of Hurts

Her
    Art,
        Her
            Heart.
Her
    Heart,
        Her
          Art.

Her
    Hurt,
        Her
         Art.
Her
    Heart,
        Her
         Hurt.

Her
    Hurt,
        Her
         Art.

Her
    Heart,
        Her
         Hurt.

Her
    Art,
        Heart,
           Heart art
                 Art heart,   Heart hurt,
                       Hurt heart.
My
    Heart
        Hurt
         Art.

Her art of a heart of hurts.

30.2.2014

LITANY OF HOPE

My Sun,

Saw long as you speak too me

Days   Days

    to   to

    Weeks   weeks

      to   to

      Months   Months

      to

      Years

And still,

Ancient words reign.
Let's tie figmented reality,
And live it laughing
Always.

1.1.2015

Ode to the Sun

My loving Sun, you inspire me to write,
I love the way you care and help others;
Invading my mind by day and through the night,
Always dreaming about the wonders of summers.

Let me compare you to the purple butterfly
You are more caring, protective and gentle;
Sun light heats the delicious peaches in July,
And summertime has flatters sentimental.

How do I love you? Let me count the ways.
I love your gentle, patient and kind heart;
Thinking of your patient love fills my days,
My love for you is from the depths of my heart.

Now I must be away with a hopeful heart.
Remember my soft words whilst we're apart.

28.9.2017

THE LOTUS FLOWER

From mud-covered waters

Untainted
Untouched

From grime

Pure
Pristine

From dirt

Bright
Beautiful

From murky waters

Clean
Crisp

Ascent
Enlightenment
Hope
Power
Against all odds
Like the lotus flower.

28.9.2018

Litany of Praise and Thanksgiving

WHO

WAS   IS   WILL

YOU

ARE

I

N

D

E

E

D

THE GREAT

I AM.

27.4.2015

O Brilliant Cherubim

Archangels

Michael

Gabriel

Raphael

Uriel

Selaphiel

Jegudiel

Barachiel

Jerahmeel

Wambui

Illuminate

My mind

With

Heavenly Knowledge.

17.2.2015

LITANY OF THE SACRED UNION

Archangel Michael
Raphael
Gabriel
Ariel
Our Guardian angels
Do you work

Archangel Michael
Raphael
Gabriel
`Ariel
Our Guardian angels
Do you work

Archangel Michael
Raphael
Gabriel
Ariel
Our Guarding Angels

Archangel Michael
Raphael
Gabriel
Ariel
Our Guarding angels

Do you work.

2.1.2015

HEART OF WORSHIP

Lord,

All

I

Want

Is

You.

All

I

Need

Is

You.

2.2.2015

THE HOUR HAS NOT YET COME

She

    Ran.

He

    Ran.

For

    the

        hour

            had

                not

                    yet

                        come.

27.6.2014

Runner Fears

Why don't you love me?

I am afraid that you will reject me
Why don't you love me?

I'm afraid of losing control
I'm afraid of being overwhelmed by emotions

Whose fears are whose?
Who is the runner?
Who is the chaser?
Who is running from whom?
Who is running?
Who is chasing?

Runner fears

Mirror Mirror
On the mount
Once upon a thousand years

I dreamed a dream of him
I saw visions of him
I knew him
He was me
I was him

Mirror Mirror
On the mount
Could it be that there's no duality?

12.30.2014

GLORY

Glory
And
Praise

This season

I choose to praise

Glory
And
Praise

Now and Always

Glory
And Praise
Glory.

12.20.2014

All I need is You

Have your way
Lord

Have your way
Christ

Have your way

All

I
Want
Is
You
Are
All
I
Need

I
Love
You

3.12.2014

HIS DAY IS NEAR

Wait for the Lord
Whose day is near
Wait for the Lord
Stay hopeful, take heart

Wait
    His day is near
            Wait
Wait
    Be strong
            Wait
Wait
    Take Heart
            Wait
His day is near
            Wait.

29.11.2017

Power of Praise

Father,

I love you.

Mother,

I thank you.

For your love for me;

I thank you.

Father,

I hear you.

Mother,

I know you are with me.

I will fear not.

For you are with me

I will give you all the praise.

Amen.

3.11.2014

YOU KEPT YOUR WORD

Lord,

You kept your word.

You are holy

You are mighty

Lord,

You kept your word.

You love me
You adore me
You love me
You adore me
You just love me

Lord,

You kept your word.

15.10.2014

THE PROPHET

Thought those days
Were long gone gone
Those those days
Were found of old old
Those those days
Were old as stone stone

Aaron
Abraham
Amos
Anna
Azaria
Barnabas
Daniel
David
Deborah
Elijah
Elisha
Enoch
Ezekiel
Gideon
Haggai
Hosea
Isaiah
Jeremiah
John the Baptist
Joshua
Malachi
Miriam
Moses

Nathan
Noah
Obadiah
Philip
Paul
Samuel
Zephaniah

Thought those days
Were long gone gone gone
Those those days
Were found of old old old
Those those days
Were old as stone.

By His stripes, you are healed
I alone know the plans
A spirit of faith quenches it
Double glory
Love love love love

Thought those days
Were long and gone
Those days are here with us
Prophets of old
Foretold their coming
The past is present
God still speaks.

16.9.2014

GOD LISTENED

I prayed
>He listened

I asked
>He listened

I cried
>He listened

I talked
>>He listened

I prayed again
>>He listened

I sung my heart out
>>He listened

I whispered
>>He listened

I continued
>Praying
>Asking
>Crying
>Talking
>Singing

Yet he had already heard.

I thank you.

Amen.

12.3.2015

PROPHECY

I am with you, fear not.
Trust him
Let your heart, be troubled not.
Trust him
You are mine, I have called you.
Trust him
Treasures, I will give you.
Trust him
To your old age,
Praise him.
Trust him
He is doing a big work
Praise him
Trust him
Double Glory
Praise him
Trust him
You are healed
Praise him
Trust him
You are victorious
Praise him
Trust him

I have called you,
You are mine.
Jeremiah 29:11
Isaiah 41:20-13
John 14:1
Isaiah 43:1-4
James 1:12
Isaiah 45:2-3
I John 4:18
Isaiah 46:3-4
1 Peter 2:24
Isaiah 25:8
Praise him.
Trust him.

The power of the prophetic word.

14.8.2014

See You Soon

See you

                        When?

Soon.

                        When?

Soon.

                     How Soon?
                     Tomorrow?
                          Today?

Soon.

                   When is soon?

Soon.

                        03.20.2017

Rest

Rest
Rest Rest
Rest Rest rest
Rest Rest Rest Rest
Rest Rest Rest Rest Rest Rest
Rest Rest Rest Rest Rest Rest Rest
Rest Rest Rest Rest Rest Rest Rest
Rest Rest Rest Rest Rest Rest Rest Rest
Rest Rest Rest Rest Rest Rest Rest Rest Rest
Rest Rest Rest Rest Rest Rest Rest Rest Rest
Rest Rest Rest Rest Rest Rest Rest Rest RestTest
Rest Rest Rest Rest Rest Rest Rest Rest Rest
Rest Rest Rest Rest Rest Rest Rest Rest
Rest Rest Rest Rest Rest Rest Rest
Rest Rest Rest Rest Rest Rest
Rest Rest Rest Rest Rest
Rest Rest Rest Rest
Rest Rest Rest
Rest Rest
Rest.

02.18.2017

Destined to Reign

Double Glory

Freedom Freedom
Love Love
Joy Joy
Peace Peace
Patience Patience
Kindness Kindnees
Faith Faith
Hope Hope
Dominion Dominion
Power Power
Majesty Majesty
Security Security
Power Power
Glory Glory

Double Glory
His Hers
Destiny.

04.03.2016

Canticle of Canticles

St. Padre Pio
St. Jude
St. Catherine
St. Anthony
St. Nicholas
St. Francis
St. Michael
St. Cecilia
St. Augustine
St. John Bosco
St. Peter

For discernment
For hope
For wisdom
For miracles
For gift giving
For piety
For fear of the Lord
For sonnets
For knowledge
For counsel
For fortitude

All the angels and saints

We implore you.

15.14.2015

DIVINE RHYTHM

```
  ?  ?   ?                          ?    ?  ?
 ?         ?                       ?          ?
?           ?                     ?            ?
?             ?                  ?             ?
 ?             ?                ?             ?
  ?             ?              ?            ?
   ?              ?    ?      ?           ?
    ?                         ?         ?
     ?                                ?
      ?                             ?
       ?                           ?
        ?                         ?
         ?                       ?
          ?                     ?
           ?                   ?
            ?                 ?
             ?               ?
              ?             ?
               ?           ?
                ?   ?
                 ? ?
                  ?
```

13.2.2015

LITANY OF AUTHENTICITY

You

In

Me

In

You

Amen.

13.2.2015

LITANY OF DIVINE PURPOSE

Where   Who   What   Why

      Am   Am   Am

       I?   I?   I?

                   Whose

                    Are

                    We?

                  JESUS.

                                    15.2.2015

Litany of Divine Love

N
O
T
H
I
N
G

L
I
K
E

T
H
E

L
O
V
E

O
F

G
O
D

13.2.2015

DID IT?

Feels
Like

It
Never
Really
Happened

It
Was
All
But
A Dream.

2.6.2018

Finally

By
The
Way

How
Have
You
Been?

Praise
The
Lord!

He
Finally
Popped
The
Question.

26.2.2018

LIFE

Waiting to be written
Waiting to be sung
Waiting to be felt
Waiting to be touched
Waiting to be recited
Waiting to be read
Waiting to be tasted
Waiting to be experienced
Waiting to be loved
Waiting to be embraced
Waiting to be remembered
Waiting to be relieved
Waiting to be lived
Life.

3.6.2018

Two in one

Venus and Jupiter
Love and Luck
Venus and Neptune
Love and Illusions
Venus and Mars
Earth and Water
Masculine and feminine
Practical and sensitive
The Fish and the Bull
Fixed and Mutable
Sun and moon
Earth and sky
Sense and Intuition
Reason and Cherish
Yin and yang
Two in one.

28.9.2018

THE TRUE VINE

Predestined
Carried the Cross
Fell
Met his mother
Met Simon
Met Veronica
Fell Again
Met the women
Fell again
Stripped
Crucified
Died
Taken from the Cross
Buried
Resurrected
Revealed
The True Vine.

28.8.2018

My God Keeps His Promises

Lord, you are a faithful God.
You promised Noah the rains would come,
And you would protect him and his family;
Your words reigned supreme.

You promised Sarah a baby,
And she conceived in her old age;
Lord, you kept your word.

You promised Abraham
He would be the father of nations;
And he had descendants
As numerous as the stars in the sky.
Lord, you kept your word.

You promised Joshua
The Children of Israel
Would see the Promised Land;
And they took possession of the Land.
Lord, your word came to pass.

You promised David,
He would be, king and he did.
Lord, you kept your word.

You promised all of humanity,

Prophet after prophet,
King after king,
Father after father,
Mother after mother,

From the days of Noah
To the days of John, the Baptist,
From Samuel to Jeremiah, and to Daniel;
From Elijah to Elisha;
From Isaiah to Jeremiah;

You promised us the coming of a Messiah
And our Savior was born on Christmas morn'.

You promised Mary, through the Angel Gabriel,
She would be blessed among women;
And she would give birth to the son of God.
And she became the Queen of queens.

You promised us
Through John, the Baptist
Our Messiah;
And the scripture was fulfilled.

You promised Elizabeth
A baby in her old age;
And John, the Baptist came into this world.

Lord, you are a faithful God.
You are not a man that you should lie.
You are an awesome God.

You promised us generations.
You promised us the comfort of the Holy Spirit.
You promised us the spirit of faith.
You promised us the spirit of truth.
You promised us the spirit of wisdom.
You promised us the spirit of hope.
You promised us the spirit of love.
You promised us the spirit of joy.
You promised us the spirit of understanding.
Your promised us the spirit of peace.
You promised us prosperous futures.

Lord, you promised us.

Your plan is for good,
Your plan is not for evil,
Your plan is to prosper us,
Your plans offer us hope and a future.

Lord, you willed it and it will be so;
I declare and, decree that your promises
Will come to pass.
In Jesus name.

Amen.

3.6.2018

He remembers his promises forever, the promise
he made, for a thousand generations.

Psalms 105:8

The Bible, New International Version

ABOUT THE AUTHOR

Nkatha Kabira is a Lecturer at the University of Nairobi, School of Law, a Fellow at the Intercontinental Academia (ICA), a postdoctoral fellow at the Ife Institute for Advanced Studies, Nigeria and a visiting scholar at STIAS in Stellenbosch, South Africa. She completed her doctoral degree at Harvard Law School (HLS) in May 2015. She has professional and research experience in several areas ranging from law and language to democracy and the legal process and to gender and the law. She lectures widely and has taught extensively both in Nairobi and at Harvard and has received awards in recognition of excellence in teaching. Prior to completing the LL.M. Program at HLS in 2008, she worked as a legal associate and pupil at Kaplan and Stratton Advocates in Nairobi, Kenya. She has worked as a research fellow at the Kenya National Commission on Human Rights, the Kenya Law Reform Commission and the Constitution of Kenya Review Commission. She holds a Bachelor of Laws degree from the University of Nairobi and a postgraduate diploma in legal practice from the Kenya School of Law. She is an Advocate of the High Court of Kenya. This is her second book of poetry.

Printed in the United States
By Bookmasters